"I'M A POSITIVE, HAPPY PERSON, GENERALLY.
THE SONGS I'VE WRITTEN ARE ABOUT
SOME BAD TIMES IN MY LIFE. I NEEDED
TO MAKE SOMETHING GOOD OUT OF
SOMETHING BAD."

AMY WINEHOUSE

1983–2011

ABDO
Publishing Company

AMY WINEHOUSE

R&B, JAZZ, & SOUL
MUSICIAN

BY DAVID ARETHA

CREDITS

Published by ABDO Publishing Company, PO Box 398166, Minneapolis, MN 55439. Copyright © 2013 by Abdo Consulting Group, Inc. International copyrights reserved in all countries. No part of this book may be reproduced in any form without written permission from the publisher. The Essential Library™ is a trademark and logo of ABDO Publishing Company.

Printed in the United States of America, North Mankato, Minnesota
062012
092012

 THIS BOOK CONTAINS AT LEAST 10% RECYCLED MATERIALS.

Editor: Rebecca Felix
Series Designer: Becky Daum

Library of Congress Cataloging-in-Publication Data
Aretha, David.
  Amy Winehouse : R&B, jazz, & soul musician / by David Aretha.
      p. cm. -- (Lives cut short)
  Includes bibliographical references and index.
  ISBN 978-1-61783-483-7
  1. Winehouse, Amy--Juvenile literature. 2. Singers--England--Biography--Juvenile literature. I. Title.
  ML3930.W535A74 2013
  782.42164092--dc23
  [B]
                                    2012001290

TABLE OF CONTENTS

1

LIVE FROM
LONDON

outh agape and eyes as wide as saucers, Amy Winehouse stood dumbfounded on a studio stage in London, England, on February 10, 2008. More than 5,000 miles (8,050 km) away in Los Angeles, California, singer Tony Bennett had just opened an envelope and announced that Winehouse's song "Rehab" had won the Grammy Award for Record of the Year for 2007. Her mother and father, Janis and Mitch, were there with her to share in her glorious moment. Winehouse hugged her parents and band

▶ A SMILING AMY WINEHOUSE CORRESPONDS VIA SATELLITE WITH THE GRAMMY AWARDS SHOW IN 2008.

members as the intimate crowd that had been invited to watch her perform began chanting her name.

It was just the beginning of a record-setting night for the soulful singer who had experienced many highs and lows in her 24 years. Winehouse's Grammy performance took place in London rather than Los Angeles, where the awards ceremony was held, because she had experienced trouble receiving approval to enter the United States. The approval had been delayed because Winehouse had recently checked herself into a London rehab center. She was making

A Special Performance

CBS, the television network that airs the Grammys, went to great lengths to share Winehouse's milestone night with her fans in the United States. Jack Sussman, the head of CBS special programming, recalled after Winehouse's death that when they learned of her troubles securing a visa, plans were made to hook into a satellite connection. Although the US government reversed an earlier decision and approved the visa two days before the show, the network and the Grammys stuck with the revised plan, figuring it would be too late for the singer to travel to Los Angeles. Sussman said he could not remember the Grammys ever going to such lengths to arrange a performance.

The result was one of the brightest moments in the short life of the talented musician. Summing up Winehouse's performance that night, Sussman said, "There is no doubt about the creative talent that woman had and what she exhibited in that moment in time."[1]

an effort to shake drug and alcohol problems that long plagued her and had affected recent performances. Arrangements were made for her to perform via satellite. When the approval was finally granted, it was too late. Winehouse was on the mend but would not make it in time to perform at the Grammys in person.

THE BIG WINNER

If Winehouse was disappointed because she would miss the walk down the red carpet in Los Angeles, she did not show it as the awards show drew near. In a statement, Winehouse said she was excited to be performing at her first Grammy Awards and continued,

> *I'd like to thank everyone for their support over the last couple of weeks. I'm really sorry I can't be there, but I appreciate that I'm being given a second chance via satellite.*[2]

It did not take long for Winehouse to steal the show once the festivities began. She was nominated for six Grammy Awards in 2008. The Record of the Year honor was the first of five Grammys Winehouse won that night. Many had expected Winehouse to win the Grammys for Best New Artist, Best Pop Vocal Album (*Back to Black*), and Best Female Pop Vocalist

Record versus Song of the Year

Winehouse's song "Rehab" won both Record of the Year and Song of the Year awards at the 2008 Grammys. Record of the Year is awarded to a single from an album and honors the work of all who collaborated on the single. This includes the band, mixers, producers, and recording staff. Song of the Year is given solely to honor the work of the songwriter.

("Rehab"). But many critics had predicted that Record and Song of the Year honors would go to singer Rihanna for "Umbrella." Winehouse pulled off the big upsets for both Record and Song of the Year with "Rehab." *Back to Black* was also up for Album of the Year. That honor was the only one she did not win. With her five wins, Winehouse tied a record previously set by four other performers for the most Grammys earned by a female singer in a single year.

DAZZLING, DEFIANT, SULTRY

Back to Black was Winehouse's second studio effort, which followed her 2003 debut album, *Frank*. "I am so proud of this album," Winehouse said of *Back to Black* and her Grammy nominations in a statement to the Associated Press. "I put my heart and soul into it, and it's wicked to be recognized in this way."[3]

But winning the awards was not Winehouse's only triumph during the telecast on February 10. Her two-song performance was dazzling,

▲ WINEHOUSE DURING HER SATELLITE PERFORMANCE AT
RIVERSIDE STUDIOS IN LONDON

especially considering the circumstances. The
time difference meant it was between 3 a.m. and
4 a.m. in London when a smiling Winehouse
took the stage in front of her parents and a cozy

crowd to perform "You Know I'm No Good" and "Rehab." The dim, intimate, cabaret-like setting suited Winehouse well.

Winehouse's well-received performance was a far cry from the erratic performances she had put on in recent months that prompted her to check into rehab. Sharing the magic with her beaming parents also set this performance apart from so many others in Winehouse's troubled life. Later remembering the night, her brother, Alex, said,

> *I'll never forget her winning the Best Record Grammy. . . . For the first time in God only knows how long, my parents were truly happy, and Amy was too. So, of course, was I. We hugged and kissed and suddenly the world melted away. . . . However, greatness, of course, isn't always accompanied by something good.[4]*

For Winehouse, few good times remained. In a tragedy that would shake the music industry, Winehouse would die of alcohol poisoning three years later at the age of 27.

▲ WINEHOUSE AND HER MOTHER, JANIS, WERE OVERJOYED AT THE NEWS OF WINEHOUSE'S MULTIPLE GRAMMY WINS.

2

BORN INTO MUSIC

hen Amy Jade Winehouse was born on September 14, 1983, it seemed as if an ordinary life awaited her. She grew up in Southgate, a tree-lined suburb in north London. Amy's father, Mitchell, known as Mitch, drove a London taxi and worked as a salesman. Her mother, Janis, was a pharmacist. But two things present in the Winehouse home would make Amy's life something other than ordinary: music and marital tension. Both influences would affect Amy as she grew older.

▶ JANIS, *BACK MIDDLE*, HOLDING AMY, MITCH, *BACK LEFT*, AND ALEX, *FRONT MIDDLE*, WITH OTHER FAMILY MEMBERS

Amy's mother described her as "a beautiful child, always busy, always curious. She was always very cheery but she was also shy. She's never been an easy child."[1] Janis remembered a time when Amy nearly choked on cellophane. On another occasion, Amy went missing in the park. Janis said of Amy,

She's reckless, very determined, and if she wants to do something she will just do it. No one can stop her once she's made her mind up, but she never thinks of the consequences.[2]

Music was in Amy's genes. Several uncles on Janis's side worked as professional jazz musicians. Amy's maternal grandmother, Cynthia, had been in a relationship with famous British tenor saxophonist and jazz club owner Ronnie Scott. Amy's older brother, Alex, played guitar. There was almost always music in the home

Southgate's Rehab Center

Southgate, the suburb where Amy grew up, lies in north London. The small suburb is mainly residential, but it bustles with shops, an underground train station, and many pubs. Southgate is also home to the Priory Hospital North London, a renowned rehabilitation facility that specializes in helping patients who have addictions. The Priory Hospital North London is a branch location of the Priory Group, which specializes in mental health care and education services throughout the United Kingdom. As an adult, Amy grew to need substance abuse rehabilitation. In 2011, she checked in at her hometown's famed clinic, just minutes from where she grew up, for a repeat try at sobriety.

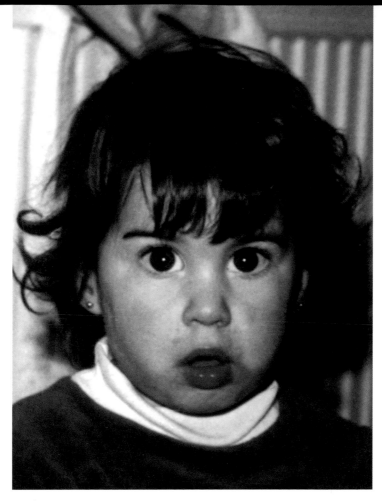

▲ AMY AT AGE TWO

and at family gatherings. Amy was exposed to many types of music growing up, including pop, classical, and blues. She listened to recordings of James Taylor, Frank Sinatra, and Sarah Vaughan, and she counted the artists among her earliest influences.

Janis remembered Amy singing "I Will Survive," a classic disco hit by Gloria Gaynor, while lying in the bathtub. Amy would break into song at school, inviting reprimands from her teachers. A neighbor recalled how Amy would pop her head out of her bedroom window, microphone in hand, and sing to the neighborhood.

NOT-SO-SECRET TROUBLES

But the Winehouse home was filled with more than music. It was also filled with turmoil caused by a known extramarital affair Amy's dad engaged in for much of Amy's childhood. For more than eight years, Mitch continued a relationship with a woman named

Troubling Revelation

In 2008, Mitch appeared on the British Broadcasting Corporation (BBC) television program *ONE Life: Rock Star Parents*. He said the extramarital affair he had been involved in during Amy's childhood was not to blame for the drug problems that affected her life and career. His comments came shortly after Amy entered a London rehabilitation clinic. Around that time, footage of her smoking what appeared to be crack cocaine had been made public. During the interview, Mitch said,

> She couldn't articulate what was wrong in words but she certainly did with her music. . . . What she is going through at the moment is terrible. . . . I think she would have found her way here one way or another without any help from me though. . . . It is easy for me to say it is my fault, and that had I been a better parent this would not have happened. But who knows whether it would or not?[3]

Jane. He admitted he made his family's life difficult during this time. "The affair was in the open," Mitch said, "and the children used to call Jane 'Daddy's work wife.' . . . The situation occurred for eight or nine years before I left home. It was difficult."[4] After divorcing Janis in 1992, Mitch moved in with Jane in 1993 and then married her in 1996.

Amy and Alex spent most of their time with Janis in Southgate after the divorce. Amy showed a defiant streak in those early years. Just how much her father's affair and her parents' strained marriage contributed to Amy's rebellious childhood is a matter of speculation. "She was always very self-willed," Mitch told *Rolling Stone* magazine in 2007. "Not badly behaved, but . . . different."[5]

AMY FINDS HER VOICE

Amy often chose to express herself through music and performance. When she was nine years old, at her grandmother's urging, Amy enrolled in the Susi Earnshaw Theatre School for formal training in the performing arts. When she was ten, Amy

The Susi Earnshaw Theatre School

The Susi Earnshaw Theatre School in London, where Amy began taking classes when she was nine, still specializes in teaching young performing-arts students. "Dare to Dream," the school encourages students on its official Web site.[6] The Web site goes on to say the school accepts no more than 15 students in any one class to give more opportunities to each pupil.

started a rap duo called Sweet 'n' Sour with a friend. Amy, who was Jewish, and the "Sour" in the tandem, later described the childhood group as "the little white Jewish Salt-N-Pepa," referring to the popular US hip-hop trio.[7] Amy's childhood friend Juliette Ashby was the other half of the duo. Although Sweet 'n' Sour recorded three songs, "Spindarella," "Glam Chicks," and "Boys . . . Who Needs Them," the group was more of a fun way for the preteens to pass time than a legitimate music act. But it did give Amy an outlet to write her own music.

Though her rap group was short lived, Amy's interest in pursuing music as a career was not. Before she experienced having songs recorded, Amy had once envisioned herself as a roller-skating waitress such as the ones who caught her eye in the film *American Graffiti*. But being part of a rap duo became just the start of Amy's future in music. "I knew I could sing," Amy said in a 2004 interview. "But I always thought everyone could sing, that everyone was born with a singing voice."[8] At age 12, Amy was accepted at the prestigious Sylvia Young Theatre School. There, she would begin to truly make her mark—for better and for worse.

▲ AMY BECAME INTERESTED IN PERFORMING AT A VERY YOUNG AGE.

3

SONGS OVER SCHOOL

When Amy submitted her application to the Sylvia Young Theatre School in London, she wrote in her essay that she dreamed of becoming famous. "It's a life-long ambition," penned the aspiring 12-year-old performer. "I want people to hear my voice and just . . . forget their troubles for five minutes."[1]

In striving to help people forget their own troubles, however, Amy may have neglected her own. Amy's time at the prestigious school would consist of moments showcasing her blossoming

▶ AMY HAD ASPIRATIONS AT A YOUNG AGE OF BEING FAMOUS ONE DAY.

talent and less-flattering ones where bad behavior overshadowed it. As Janis explained, "She was very bright, but she was always messing around."[2]

Although Amy often sang growing up, the extent of her talent was not apparent until her time at the Sylvia Young Theatre School. Amy's father recalls being blown away by a recital Amy was in while there. "I thought she'd just be acting. But then she came out on stage and started singing, and I couldn't believe it," he said. "I never knew she could sing like that."[3] Amy's acting got noticed as well. Amy appeared with other Sylvia Young students in a 1997 episode of the British cult television comedy *The Fast Show*. In the episode, Amy played a student putting on a play. During the play, a disgruntled father objects to his son's acting and jumps onstage to take over the boy's role alongside Amy, who acts stunned. Even then, she stood out.

By the time she was in her mid-teens, however, Amy was far more interested in her own music than her education. Her musical interest was influenced by jazz greats from earlier eras, including composer and pianist Thelonious Monk and singer Dinah Washington. "To hear subtle music like that, like a trio could give more to me than a big band, that's when I learned about less is more," she said.[4] At the same time, Amy also liked the music of rappers such as Mos Def, Nas, and Busta Rhymes. As she developed as an artist, Amy combined elements of jazz and rap into her music, creating a unique style that was her own.

Amy began playing her brother's guitar and then bought her own at age 13. She began writing her own songs approximately a year later, and the lyrics were frequently filled with pain. This was also around the time Amy discovered marijuana. "I do suffer from depression, I suppose, which isn't unusual," Amy explained years later to an interviewer. "You know, a lot of people do."[5] Because Amy had an older brother whom she saw going through life experiences sooner, it was possible she went through teenage angst a bit early. "I think because I had an older brother, I did a lot of that 'Oh, life's so depressing' stuff before I was even 12," she said. "That's when I would be reading J. D. Salinger—or whatever my brother read— and feeling frustrated."[6]

Teenage Dreams

In December 2010, seven months before Amy's death, a collection of notes and lyrics believed to be written by Amy during her teen years was found in a London trash can. The items on her to-do list included: "Buy flat in London," "Get gym membership," and "Live like the bombshell I really am."[7] She also wanted to get her teeth fixed, acquire or use a treadmill, and buy a sunbed.

REBELLION

Around the same time she began writing songs, Amy's time at the Sylvia Young Theatre School came to an end. Sources contain conflicting reports about why she did not finish her studies there. Amy was impatient with the regimen of education, which is the reason she cited for not staying in school. Students who misbehaved at school would go on report. Then the teachers would have to sign pieces of paper after each class confirming the students attended and comment on their behavior. "I didn't like being told what to do. I was on report all the time," Amy said. "It gets to you after a while. . . . So I left."[8] However, *Rolling Stone* reported she was expelled two years after enrolling, at age 14, for piercing her own nose and for her "general slackeritude."[9] Other reports confirm she got in trouble for such offenses but claim it was Amy's decision to drop out at 14. Though sources vary as to whether she was kicked out or dropped out, most claim that leaving school was not ultimately Amy's decision.

Amy began showing a rebellious spirit outside of school as well. At 15, she got her first tattoo. This act was illegal, as 18 is the legal age to get a tattoo in the United Kingdom (UK). The tattoo was an image of cartoon character Betty Boop, located on Amy's back. It was the first of many inked images that would eventually adorn Amy's petite body. Getting the tattoo was a prime example of the defiant nature Amy had developed by this time. "My parents pretty much realized that I would do whatever I wanted," she said, "and that was it, really."[10]

In 1998, when she was 15 and 16, Amy briefly went back to school, this time to the BRIT School for Performing Arts and Technology in London, which the British Record Industry Trust helps support. But Amy did not stay at the BRIT School either. By 16, she had left school for good.

The First of Many Tattoos

In a 2007 interview with *Rolling Stone*, Amy said she decided to get her first tattoo when she was 15 simply because she liked tattoos. Amy continued adorning her body in the following years. By the time she was 24, Amy had at least 12 tattoos, and more would follow. Among the most striking inked artwork was an anchor and the words "Hello Sailor" on her midriff, two pinup girls on her right arm, and a horseshoe with the words "Daddy's Girl" near her left shoulder. Other tattoos included a lightning bolt, a feather, and a bird surrounded by flowers, branches, music notes, and the words "Never Clip My Wings." The name "Cynthia" was added near the pinup girl tattoos on Amy's arm in memory of her beloved grandmother. In another tribute, Amy had the possessive of her future husband's name—"Blake's"—inked on her chest near her heart. When asked by *Rolling Stone* whether she ever thought of covering up a tattoo in regret, Amy replied, "I don't regret anything."[11]

▲ THE REBELLIOUSNESS AMY DEVELOPED IN HER TEENS
LASTED THROUGHOUT THE REST OF HER LIFE.

After leaving the BRIT School, Amy lived at
home with her mom while working several odd
jobs. She continued writing music and playing
guitar with jazz leanings, and she honed her

singing talents, occasionally playing locally. It was during these middle teenage years that Amy landed her first real job in the entertainment industry—a night gig as a show business reporter for the World Entertainment News Network (WENN). But reporting on celebrities was not precisely where Amy wanted to be in the industry. So while she was doing just that for WENN, she was also using her rich, mature voice to front a London jazz band. The talented teenage Amy had time, and immense talent, on her side.

Famous BRITs

The BRIT School Amy briefly attended in 1998 is prestigious and famed for having schooled many talented performers. Although her time there was brief, Amy made an impression. Her music teacher at the BRIT School recalled Amy was quite popular with fellow students. Other famous BRIT students include pop sensations Leona Lewis and Adele.

———•◆•———

4

DISCOVERED

When Winehouse was 16, a fortunate break came her way. Tyler James was a former Sylvia Young schoolmate and on-and-off boyfriend who was also a singer. James offered Winehouse studio time to cut a demo. "I didn't believe he'd actually let me do it," Winehouse later told *Rolling Stone*. "I just didn't get why he would be so willing to help me, because I didn't think it was special to be able to sing."[1]

The breaks continued for Winehouse after the demo was created. James passed the demo

▶ WINEHOUSE OCCASIONALLY PLAYED IN LOCAL CLUBS BEFORE HER BIG BREAK.

on to his record label, A&R, which was looking for a jazz vocalist. The result was a contract with management company 19 Entertainment Ltd. in 2002. Entertainment mogul Simon Fuller, creator of the popular singing-contest television show *American Idol,* headed the company. Under this management, Winehouse was signed to record label Island Records/Universal.

Winehouse acquired management and a recording contract for her powerful and unique vocal abilities. She also impressed with her mature songwriting. Large, well-known company EMI Music Publishing took notice. EMI signed Winehouse to a publishing contract shortly after she landed her first recording deal. If any other artist wanted to record or perform a song Winehouse composed, he or she would have to pay EMI, which would then share a part of that fee with Winehouse. At just 18, Winehouse was ready

Recording versus Publishing Contract

A musical artist who lands a record deal signs a recording contract. With this legal agreement, the artist commits to making a record or series of records for the record company. The record company will sell and promote the records and give the artist a share of the profits. A publishing contract publishes, manages, and protects a musical composition's rights for a certain period of time. Other artists wanting to perform or record a composition protected under the contract during that time pays the music publishing company. The music publishing company shares the profits, in the form of royalties, with the songwriter.

to spread her wings and begin working on her first album. She was also ready to move out of her mother's house.

MOVING UP— AND OUT

Shortly after her first EMI paycheck arrived, Winehouse moved into a London flat, or apartment, with her lifelong friend and former Sweet 'n' Sour partner Ashby. The two shared a flat in London for two years. Winehouse and Ashby had met in nursery school at age four and were practically inseparable during their elementary-school years. Their parents tried to keep the

Superior Songwriting

Songwriter Stefan Skarbek first met Winehouse when she was 14. He recognized her songwriting talent immediately. "When she wrote music, the best way I can describe her is she was like an owl and a porcelain doll, she was so wise, but then so young and innocent," he said. "I knew she was incredible—we didn't even write lyrics, just messed around on a piano for five minutes and then she'd go in a room, come up with genius lyrics and amazing melodies."[2] Skarbek was not the only one who noticed Winehouse's talent for penning standout lyrics. Throughout her career, songwriters, musicians, music companies, and academies would all praise Winehouse for her abilities. Skarbek, who would cowrite a number of songs with Winehouse in later years, summed up the influence of Winehouse's lyrics: "She opened the gateway to so many other artists and in my view, she changed the whole paradigm of music," he said. "I think she made it possible . . . for the other artists that have come through to exist and put some truth and honesty back in music again."[3]

▲ CAMDEN IN NORTH LONDON, WHERE WINEHOUSE AND
CLOSE FRIEND ASHBY RENTED AN APARTMENT

mischievous pair apart, but the efforts failed.
Ashby said,

> We were always getting up to some sort [of]
> mischief . . . when we got to secondary school
> our mums went up to the school and begged for
> us not to be put in the same class together . . .
> [but] that didn't stop us being best friends.[4]

Moving in together as teenagers was the start of an exciting time in both their lives. But freedom, spending money, and an inside view of the vibrant London music scene resulted in plenty of temptations, including drug use, which the young friends partook in. Winehouse and Ashby had highs and lows living together, and although temptations ultimately took their toll, the friendship survived. Ashby recalled of her flat with Winehouse,

> *We had two of the best years of our lives there together, with memories that will never be erased. But unfortunate circumstances began taking her life and our friendship out of control, although through all the pain and disturbing experiences that followed, we always remained right by each other's side whenever we needed each other.*[5]

ECLECTIC TALENTS

As she turned her notebook pages of songs into her first album, Winehouse had the good fortune of working with some talented producers in the studio who helped cowrite a few tracks. Producer Salaam Remi's roots were in hip-hop and reggae, and his production résumé included longtime work with hip-hop group the Fugees. Scottish producer Jimmy Hogarth grew up listening to hard rockers including Led Zeppelin and AC/DC before turning his tastes toward soul and R&B. The acclaimed producers and Winehouse's unique, distinctively rich and soulful jazz voice made for an interesting— and winning—mix. A breakthrough record emerged that would be named for its honest and sometimes abrupt lyrics. Its title: *Frank*.

———•◆•———

▲ WINEHOUSE'S LYRICS CAPTURED EMOTIONS HONESTLY, AND HER POWERFUL VOICE GAVE THEM STRONG EFFECT.

5

FRANK

No one had any idea how big a splash Winehouse would make—on and off the stage—before *Frank* was released in the United Kingdom on October 20, 2003. When critics heard Winehouse's soulful voice and the pulsating drums on the opening track, they took notice.

"Winehouse's lyrics are almost as remarkable as that voice," wrote online magazine *MusicOMH* critic John Murphy. "There's so much maturity and depth here that it's hard to believe that she

▸ WINEHOUSE IN DECEMBER 2003

isn't yet out of her teens."[1] Matt Walton of the BBC raved,

> *Imagine a voice as distinctive as Dinah Washington or Billie Holiday. Imagine personal lyrics which paint images of a young woman's life in London. Got that? That's pretty much 19-year-old Amy Winehouse's debut LP: classic jazz crooning dirtied with her other influences.*[2]

Frank's Legacy

Winehouse's first album, *Frank*, seemed to get better with age. The album reentered the UK charts in January 2007, almost three years after it was released, and stayed there for much of the year. The resurgence in *Frank*'s popularity happened on the heels of the 2006 release of Winehouse's album *Back to Black*. *Frank* was released in the United States for the first time in 2007, and it debuted at Number 61 on the *Billboard* chart in December.

After Winehouse's passing in 2011, her albums once again began flying off the shelves. In the first 36 hours following Winehouse's death, nearly 8,000 copies of *Frank* were downloaded in the United States. *Frank* moved higher on both the UK charts (to number three) and US charts (to number 33) in August 2011.

HONEST, UNIQUE LYRICS

Winehouse's songs on her debut album were praised for being so personal. Her rich voice wove original, unguarded stories that felt beyond her years. Wrote Beccy Lindon of the *Guardian*,

> *Winehouse sounds as if she has performed a thousand times*

in smoky jazz clubs. . . . 'Take the Box' is a stunningly soulful tale . . . and 'You Send Me Flying' does just that, thanks to a colossal vocal talent. . . . It's hard not to hear the honesty and soul that resonates throughout this album.[3]

The first track on *Frank*, titled "Stronger Than Me," includes the lyrics, "Don't you know you're supposed to be the man / Not pale in comparison to who you think I am."[4] "What It Is About Men" is a self-deprecating slow groove and "I Heard Love Is Blind" tells the tale of cheating with her boyfriend's look-alike. While promoting the album, Winehouse revealed the lyrics were based largely on her experiences with one man. Apparently, the album was a little too honest for him. Winehouse recalled, "He did say to me, 'How would you feel if I did this to you?'"[5] This exchange epitomized Winehouse's future life. Her desire to say and do whatever she wanted sometimes had mixed results, including admiration from fans and critics and devastation to herself and her loved ones.

Winehouse's music career looked promising in 2004. *Frank* was nominated for two BRIT Awards that year. The BRIT Awards are the annual British Record Industry music awards, similar to the Grammy Awards in the United

▲ Winehouse promoting the BRIT Awards in
January 2004

States. The album was also nominated for the
2004 Mercury Music Prize, which is given to
the top British or Irish release. While *Frank*
did not win the Mercury Music Prize or
BRIT Awards, the honors kept coming for
Winehouse and her album. By February 2004,
Frank, which had debuted in October 2003 at
Number 60 on the UK Top 75, had climbed to
Number 13. "Stronger Than Me," the first of

four singles released, won the Ivor Novello Award for Best Contemporary Song on May 3, 2004.

SPEAKING OUT

While *Frank* was getting plenty of recognition, it seemed Winehouse was not particularly proud of her first album. At times, she spoke as if she would have liked to do it all over. She admitted badmouthing her own music was detrimental:

> **Ivor Novello Award**
>
> The Ivor Novello Award is one of the most prestigious awards a British song-writer can win. The Ivors, as they are called, have been presented by the British music writing community for more than 50 years. Past winners include Paul McCartney, Elton John, and Quincy Jones.

> *I know it's a terrible thing for someone to come out and say they hate their own music. It's the worst thing you can do. My album isn't [crap]. If I heard someone else singing like me, I would buy it in a heartbeat.*[6]

Winehouse blasted the marketing and promotion of her debut. She called out failed publicity efforts as making a negative impact. "The marketing was [screwed up], the promotion was terrible. Everything was a shambles," she said.[7] "I've never heard the album start to finish," Winehouse told London newspaper the *Observer* in a story published more than three months after *Frank*'s release.[8]

At other times, Winehouse spoke positively about the originality of her songs, the confidence that her producer Remi brought out in her, and her penchant for dealing with serious issues in a lighthearted way. "I have written about times in my life that have given me trouble," she said in an April 2004 interview, "and there are points on the album where I am really upset and really angry. I'll always put a punch line in there and I'll always make it funny."[9]

Winehouse's stubbornness and unpredictability appeared in the often-abrasive things she said onstage and to interviewers. Her manager Nick Godwin did not seem to mind, though. "I'm used to this. She can be very frustrating. But I don't have an issue with her frankness," he said. "She's a real artist who's going to make records for years to come."[10]

Though she badmouthed the debut of *Frank* and was showing signs of erratic behavior, there was no doubt Winehouse was embracing her role in the spotlight. In 2004, she said her performances

Musical Pride

Following the release of *Frank*, Winehouse said music gave her dignity. "That's the one area in my life where I can hold my head up and say, 'No one can touch me.' 'Cause no one can touch me!"[11]

▲ ALTHOUGH SLIGHT MEDIA NEGATIVITY SURROUNDING WINEHOUSE'S BEHAVIOR WAS BEGINNING BY 2004, SHE WORKED HARD TO GIVE FANS GOOD PERFORMANCES.

were "a case of me wanting to please the crowd by giving the songs their just due every night, mainly because I'm really, really proud of them."[12] Winehouse's erratic behavior may have been due to other prominent forces that began shaking up her life the same time as her debut: love and substance abuse.

6

LOVE AND TROUBLE

The year of *Frank*'s UK release marked another significant event in Winehouse's life. Winehouse met former video production assistant Blake Fielder-Civil, the man who would be her future husband and muse, at a London bar in 2003. If her first album was the turning point in Winehouse's music career, many would argue meeting Fielder-Civil was the turning point in her personal life.

Fielder-Civil, a fellow Brit two years older than Winehouse, swept her off her feet.

▶ WINEHOUSE AND BLAKE FIELDER-CIVIL HAD AN INTENSE RELATIONSHIP FROM THE BEGINNING.

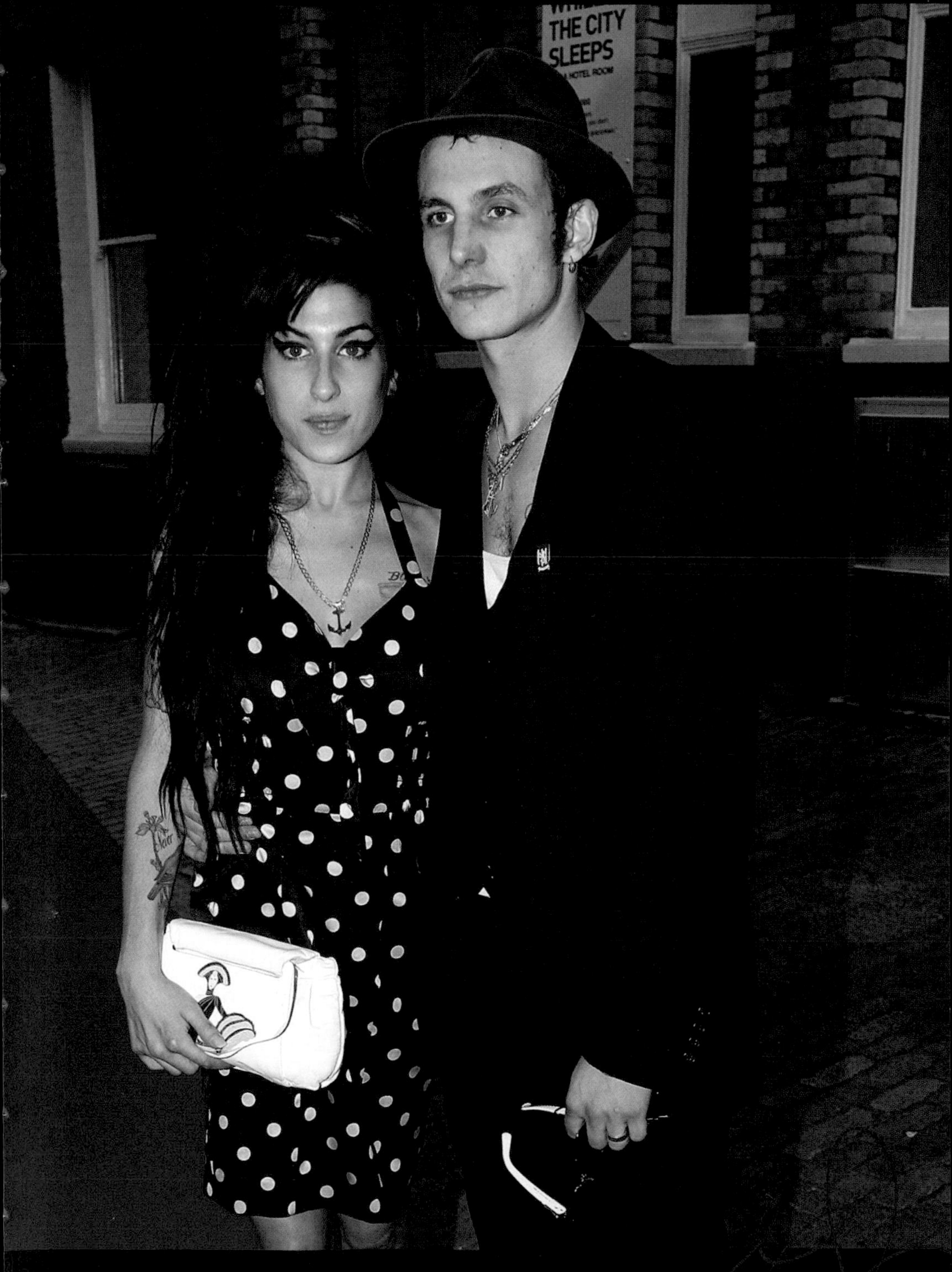
THE CITY
SLEEPS

Winehouse fell passionately in love with Fielder-Civil and remained so for most of her short life.

Winehouse gave herself completely to the romance and solidified her devotion by getting a tattoo of a shirt pocket with the word "Blake's" inked on her chest. She penned songs delving into the emotions—both dreamy and disturbing—of her first serious love. It was an inspired time in Winehouse's songwriting career, resulting in much of the music that would comprise her next and most successful album, *Back to Black*.

However, a hard-to-ignore darkness developed around Winehouse as her relationship with Fielder-Civil grew. Their relationship was bumpy and took its toll on her. Fielder-Civil had problems with substance abuse. Together, the couple indulged heavily in alcohol and drugs, sending them both down a dark path.

Troubling Muse

The intense relationship between Winehouse and Fielder-Civil never left her short of inspiration or material for her writing. Their eventual breakups, in that regard, led to some of her best work, including the heartbreaking lyrics from *Back to Black* songs that resonated with her fans. After she and Fielder-Civil got back together in the spring of 2007, *Entertainment Weekly* asked Winehouse whether she would still be able to produce heartfelt, distraught lyrics. Winehouse affirmed, "I've still got loads left over from the last breakup. It's never gonna be butterflies and sunsets."[1]

DOWNFALLS DURING A RISE TO FAME

Touring in support of *Frank* took Winehouse from several intimate venues close to home to some of the world's biggest music festivals. She performed in Glastonbury, England; Rotterdam, Netherlands; and Montreal, Canada.

But while many of her performances were riveting, Winehouse was beginning to show signs of the alcohol- and drug-fueled instability that would eventually characterize her life and career. She showed up to some shows too intoxicated to complete an entire set. By 2005, Winehouse's substance use, relationship with Fielder-Civil, and negative behavior began getting as much attention in the media as her music.

Mixed Perceptions

Sarah Hurley, the owner of the Good Mixer pub in London, was a friend of Winehouse's for 12 years. She remembers Winehouse as kind and personable, despite what was portrayed in the media. "Even when she became a star and would come in with her two bouncers," Hurley recalled, "she was always polite and down-to-earth and happy to sign autographs if fans asked. . . . She was never a diva."[2]

Winehouse, Hurley recalled, was a talented pool player who could beat all of the bar's regulars. Hurley also noticed the special bond between Winehouse and Fielder-Civil. Hurley noted, "She and Blake would come in together, and in their happiest days you could not meet two people more in love." Although Winehouse drank plenty of alcohol in the pub, Hurley recalled, "I never ever saw her out of control, like in some pictures."[3]

▲ Being together escalated Fielder-Civil's and Winehouse's drug and alcohol abuse.

"Biggest Mistake"

Winehouse had stumbled into drugs and alcohol when she was a teenager. But Fielder-Civil admitted he introduced her to hard drugs in a way she had never been exposed to them before. "I made the biggest mistake of my life by taking heroin in front of her," Fielder-Civil later said in a 2008 interview. "I introduced her to heroin, crack cocaine, and self-harming. I feel more than guilty."[4] At one point during their relationship, Fielder-Civil thought Winehouse had died in his arms after ingesting too many drugs. He said he administered mouth-to-mouth aid in an effort to keep her alive.

Along with, or maybe due to, the chaos of their drug and alcohol abuse, Winehouse and Fielder-Civil had many breakups. In 2006, while the couple was split up, Winehouse dated chef and musician Alex Claire, who later sold a racy story about their time together to a London tabloid. That year, Winehouse lost her beloved grandmother Cynthia, whom she credited with encouraging her to become a singer. Cynthia died of lung cancer, and Winehouse's father said the death might have contributed to Winehouse's growing depression. It was during Winehouse's touring in 2006 when friends, her father, and members of her management team began urging her to enter a rehabilitation facility to get her life back on track. In what became a premise for her future hit song, "Rehab," Winehouse refused.

▲ WINEHOUSE'S SIGNATURE BEEHIVE AND WINGED
BLACK EYELINER

During this time, Winehouse lost considerable
weight and transformed her look. She had always
had a distinct style, wearing fifties-style ensembles
in bright, splashy colors and donning heavy
eyeliner. But during these especially rocky times,
Winehouse incorporated another eye-catching
element, adopting what would become her

signature beehive hairdo. "The more insecure I feel, the bigger my beehive gets," she once said.[5]

DEPTHS OF DEPRESSION

Winehouse's troubles seemed to spiral more and more out of control as she worked on her second album, *Back to Black*. In various interviews surrounding its October 27, 2006, release, Winehouse admitted to numerous problems. She said she suffered from manic depression, had an eating disorder, and had engaged in self-injury. "I do drink a lot," Winehouse said. "I think it's symptomatic of my depression. I'm manic depressive; I'm not an alcoholic, which sounds like an alcoholic in denial."[6]

Winehouse's problems were not hers alone. Abusing drugs and alcohol and self inflicting bodily harm created a dangerous and vicious cycle for Winehouse and beau Fielder-Civil. Winehouse's father, Mitch, said Fielder-Civil once

Unique Sense of Style

After becoming a celebrity, Winehouse became a fashion trendsetter beyond her signature beehive hairdo and dramatic eyeliner. A commemorative edition of *Time* magazine published after her death, *Amy Winehouse, 1983–2011: A Tribute*, listed ten of Winehouse's fashion contributions. These include leopard-skin, nautical elements such as sailor tattoos and anchor necklaces, 1950s-inspired looks such as vibrant-colored bowling shirts, gaudy gold jewelry, satin ballet shoes, underwear as outerwear, mixing clashing prints, and retro minidresses in flower prints.

▲ AMID PERFORMING AND RELEASING A NEW ALBUM,
WINEHOUSE WAS STRUGGLING WITH DEPRESSION IN 2006.

told him why the couple chose to self-mutilate.
"He explained to me that when they're going into
[drug] withdrawal, if they cut themselves, it takes

away the pain," Mitch told the *Times* of London.[7]

During those dark and troubling times, Winehouse was also juggling tour dates and spending time in the studio, where she poured the gamut of her emotions into her music. The result of her time in the studio was *Back to Black*, which turned out to be the crowning achievement of her career. But despite her musical success, Winehouse's personal life was falling to pieces.

Plea for Help

Fielder-Civil's parents, Giles and Georgette, made an impassioned plea in August 2007 for their son and Winehouse to give up their drug use and seek help. "I think they both need to get medical help," Georgette told the BBC, "before one of them, if not both of them, eventually [dies]."[8]

7

BACK TO BLACK

Both critically and commercially, *Back to Black* exceeded Winehouse's successful debut release, *Frank*, from three years earlier. A reporter for the *Washington Post* wrote,

Winehouse isn't just a bar singer with an easily packaged back story. She's one of the most exciting newish arrivals on the post-millennial R&B scene—a 23-year-old artist with a knack for writing blunt, confessional relationship songs that are full of ache, attitude and humor.[1]

▸ WINEHOUSE SINGING HER HIT SONG "REHAB" IN JUNE 2007

Winehouse's track "Rehab" was getting most of the attention. The song was officially released on October 23, 2006, days before the album hit store shelves. The song painted the very real situation of Winehouse's needing to go to rehab and her unfortunate refusal. On the track, Winehouse croons, "They tried to make me go to rehab / I said, 'No, no, no.'"[2] The song does not spell out who "they" refers to, but it likely included her management, friends, and family. She says she does not want to go to rehab because "there's nothing you can teach me" there. Other lyrics are ambiguous. "I don't ever wanna

Back to Black Accolades

In addition to winning five 2008 Grammy Awards and being the biggest-selling album in the United Kingdom in 2007, *Back to Black* was named the Number 1 album of 2007 by *Time* magazine. The album placed high on many other publications' best-of lists as well, including Number 2 best on *Entertainment Weekly*'s The Best (and Worst) Albums of 2007, and Number 3 album on the *New York Times*'s list of top music that year. The album continued gaining accolades many years past its debut. In 2009, *Back to Black* was named Number 20 on Rolling Stone's 100 Best Albums of the '00s list, recognizing top music from the first decade of the 2000s. The week after Winehouse's death, the album reentered the *Billboard* chart for top 200 albums at Number 9. Individual songs were given special recognition as well. In total, the album produced five hit singles: "Rehab," "You Know I'm No Good," "Back to Black," "Tears Dry on Their Own," and "Love Is a Losing Game."

drink again," she sings, adding, "I just need a friend." She further declares in the song, "And it's not just my pride / It's just 'til these tears have dried."[3]

Troubling as it may have been, boldly calling attention to, and even celebrating, her denial of the rehabilitation she desperately needed seemed to make Winehouse even more famous. "Rehab" became Winehouse's signature song and shot up the charts on both sides of the Atlantic Ocean. But "Rehab" was not the only track on *Back to Black* that was noticed. *Entertainment Weekly* named "You Know I'm No Good" the second-best song of 2007. A *Billboard* magazine reviewer raved that the song, the album's second single release, "is as hip-hop as it is blues with a chomping breakbeat. . . . By album's end, you're left just like Winehouse—spent but wanting more."[4] The title song, "Back to Black," was deemed "one more in an album of performances that certify the 23-year-old Winehouse as an undeniable master," in an iTunes review.[5] Winehouse's second album was going to become a worldwide hit.

THROWBACK SOUND

Winehouse had known exactly where she wanted to go with the overall sound of her second release.

She had long been a fan of rock and roll's early girl groups and wanted *Back to Black* to stand out as a throwback to the doo-wop and bebop sounds of the 1950s and 1960s. Referring to the vast differences between *Back to Black* and her first album, *Frank,* Winehouse noted,

> *I didn't want to play the jazz thing up too much again. I was bored of complicated chord structures and needed something more direct. I'd been listening to a lot of girl groups from the '50s and '60s. I liked the simplicity of that stuff. It just gets to the point. So I started thinking about writing songs in that way.*[6]

As she scrawled lyrics to the songs for *Back to Black*, Winehouse wanted humor to go hand in hand with the serious stuff. "You've got to get that in there," she said. "Life is funny and sad, sometimes both at the same time."[7]

Frank producer Remi stayed on board for production work for *Back to Black,* pooling his considerable talents with producer Mark Ronson. A *Rolling Stone* review praised Remi's and Ronson's ability to turn classic sounds into something new.

▲ Fielder-Civil and Winehouse in June 2007, just weeks after they married

Marriage and Mayhem

Winehouse's second album was topping the UK charts and selling well all over the globe. It seemed some things in her personal life were on an upswing as well. Winehouse and Fielder-Civil were back together after a 2006 breakup, and on May 18, 2007, they snuck off to Miami, Florida, and got married. According to marriage clerk

Sammy Calixte, "They came in to get married and they were alone. . . . When I pronounced them man and wife, they hugged and kissed."[8]

After the ceremony, Winehouse and Fielder-Civil were coy with reporters about whether they had gotten married. But the same day, Winehouse's publicist confirmed to *People* magazine the couple had indeed married. Fielder-Civil confirmed it himself days later when he changed the status on his account on social networking Web site Myspace from "single" to "married." In a concert in London in early June, Winehouse said to the audience, "I don't know if you heard, but I just got married to the best man in the world."[9]

But despite her success on the music charts and her new marital status, Winehouse's drug and alcohol abuse continued to negatively affect her professional and personal life. On August 23, a bloodied Winehouse was photographed alongside Fielder-Civil at a London hotel. Some suspected a fight between the two, but Winehouse said she had been cutting herself and

Short Engagement

Winehouse's engagement to Fielder-Civil lasted one month in 2007. Fielder-Civil proposed to Winehouse with a diamond ring from famed jewelry store Tiffany's in April of that year and they were married the next month. Winehouse said she had hopes of being with Fielder-Civil for the rest of her life.

▲ WINEHOUSE AND FIELDER-CIVIL ON AUGUST 24, 2007,
THE DAY AFTER THE HOTEL INCIDENT THAT WAS EITHER A
FIGHT OR INTERVENTION BETWEEN THE TWO

was about to take drugs when her husband came
to her rescue. Fielder-Civil had a slightly different
story:

> We had a mad argument, we was out of our
> nuts, and I smashed a bottle and took a chunk
> out of myself. She just looked at me and out

*of fear or love or whatever it was and, out of
some weird sense of loyalty, she did the same
thing to herself.*[10]

Whichever situation was true, both versions
of the story were disturbing and exemplified
dangerous behaviors.

That same month, Winehouse canceled a
number of shows on her European tour, officially
citing exhaustion and poor health. Publicist
Tracey Miller told *People* magazine it was a
case of the star's time and energy being spread
thin. "She has done hundreds of shows and
promotional appearances in the last year, often
working 16-hour days. It's bound to catch up
with anybody," she said.[11] However, Winehouse
divulged another reason. She told German
magazine *Stern* she had been hospitalized after
"overdosing on a mix of substances, including
heroin, ecstasy, cocaine, ketamine, and alcohol."[12]

As severe as her problems with drugs and
alcohol had become, they were not the only
problems that plagued Winehouse. "I went
through every eating disorder you can have,"
she said. "A little bit of anorexia, a little bit of
bulimia."[13] Both conditions take a terrible toll on
the physical and mental health of an individual.
Anorexia, an eating disorder characterized by an

aversion to food or fear of gaining weight, can lead to side effects such as brittle bones, hair loss, and anemia. The effects of the binge eating and vomiting associated with bulimia include organ damage, tooth decay, and constant stomach pain.

Winehouse's father confirmed her problems with eating disorders in an October 2007 interview. He said that although Winehouse was eating, her eating disorder had not been completely dealt with. It seemed that along with drug and alcohol abuse, Winehouse's problems with eating disorders were dangers she could not move past.

Then, in November 2007, Fielder-Civil was arrested for attacking a British pub manager, whom he then tried to bribe. Fielder-Civil offered the pub manager $400,000 to keep quiet about the attack. Fielder-Civil would be held in jail for approximately nine months awaiting trial, which was longer than he and Winehouse had even been married.

Newly Wed and Behind Bars

Fielder-Civil served time in Pentonville Prison in the London borough of Islington for his 2007 assault on a pub manager. Winehouse and Fielder-Civil's relationship appeared to continue while he was imprisoned. Fielder-Civil's drug problems also seemed to continue in jail. During his sentence, Fielder-Civil was admitted to a prison hospital for a suspected heroin overdose. Shortly after, Winehouse appeared in public with a small teardrop drawn with eyeliner under her left eye.

REHAB, FINALLY

Winehouse's alcohol and substance abuse reached the point where there was no more saying no to rehab. British media reported Winehouse checked into rehabilitation facilities twice in 2007, but she left both times before her treatment was completed. While her attempts to get clean were failing, Winehouse's career success continued. That same year, *Back to Black* was the Number 1 selling album in the United Kingdom with 1.85 million copies sold. The 2008 Grammy Awards, which honored music from 2007, were coming up in February. Winehouse had experienced a sensational year musically—the Grammys would be a big night. Winehouse checked into rehab again on January 24, 2008. "She has come to understand that she requires specialist treatment to continue her ongoing recovery from drug addiction and prepare for her planned appearance at the Grammy Awards," noted a statement from Universal Music Group when Winehouse entered rehab for the third time.[14]

Fans wondered how fit Winehouse would be for the Grammys. In an interview for *Blender* magazine published in the fall of 2007 with reporter Jody Rosen, Winehouse kept falling

▲ A BLONDE WINEHOUSE WITH HER FATHER, MITCH, ONE WEEK BEFORE SHE ENTERED REHAB IN JANUARY 2008

asleep. The reporter painted a grim picture of an overworked, overtired star suffering from substance abuse. Rosen described the interview,

> *[Winehouse's] words are slurred, her eyelids drooping. Her head wobbles into a nod. She falls asleep for a second, wakes up with a start, mutters and drops off again. The smoldering cigarette in her left hand falls to the floor.[15]*

It seemed Winehouse's substance abuse problems were eclipsing her time in the spotlight.

———◆———

8

FAST LIVING

inehouse's 2008 Grammy Awards performance via satellite marked the beginning of a busy two-year schedule of performances that were sometimes overshadowed by her substance abuse. Winehouse's live shows could be epic, but they could also be cut short when she was incoherent. Two days after Winehouse's five wins at the Grammys, her mother appeared on a British radio program and insisted her daughter was finally cleaning up her act. "She's on the road to recovery," Janis said of her daughter's

▸ WINEHOUSE WAS OUT OF REHAB AND KEEPING UP A BUSY SCHEDULE BY FEBRUARY 2008.

substance-abuse problems.[1] However, it was a premature declaration.

Two months later, on April 25, 2008, Winehouse was arrested and detained overnight for allegedly head-butting a 38-year-old man outside a London pub at 3:20 a.m. on April 23. Winehouse was arrested by appointment, meaning she voluntarily went in for questioning. She was not charged with assault for the incident, but the incident was kept on her record. The same day, April 25, Fielder-Civil had a court appearance for his November 2007 arrest. Winehouse did not attend her husband's court hearing that day.

Less than two weeks later, on May 7, Winehouse was arrested again in connection with a video that had surfaced in January, showing her doing drugs at a party in her London home. The video showed her inhaling fumes from a small pipe. Winehouse went to court for the incident, but she was not charged with an offense. But 34-year-old Johnny Blagrove, the man who sold the video to a London tabloid, was sentenced to two years in jail for selling drugs to Winehouse and other celebrities. He was charged with selling cocaine and ecstasy.

Though Winehouse was released without being charged with an offense, the incident was yet another blemish on her growing list of public-relations nightmares. While Winehouse had narrowly avoided several legal charges, her incarcerated husband pleaded guilty in court in early June 2008 for the pub manager attack and attempted bribery incident. Although these incidents created bad publicity, Winehouse's behavior did not yet seem to be heavily interfering with her fan base.

Spending in Excess

After *Back to Black* hit it big, Winehouse made millions of dollars. According to *Amy Winehouse, 1983–2011: A Tribute*, she left behind a $10 million fortune when she died. She also spent a fortune while she was alive. According to the tribute magazine, Winehouse spent $4 million on her house in London. Inside the house, she spent $16,000 for a sweet shop that included a cotton-candy machine and a Slush Puppie maker. She also spent $1 million on houses for her parents, $3.2 million on clothes and shoes, $2.5 million on drugs and alcohol for herself and her friends, and $800,000 on rehab.

ON TOUR AND IN TROUBLE

On June 27, 2008, Winehouse gave one of her sharpest post-Grammy performances when she sang in London's Hyde Park at a special event honoring South African leader Nelson Mandela's ninetieth birthday. Though her track record had fans and critics speculating about whether she would even show up, Winehouse looked and sounded great during group opening and closing numbers. She also dazzled during a two-song solo set in the middle of the program, which also featured actors Will Smith and Jada Pinkett Smith, and singers Leona Lewis and Annie Lennox.

But Winehouse continued to struggle. One week later, a photo surfaced of her drinking wine during her performance at Madrid's Rock in Rio music festival. Later that summer, Winehouse was hospitalized after fainting in her north London home. As Winehouse's life was spinning out of control the summer of 2008, Fielder-Civil was still behind bars, which added to Winehouse's turmoil. In July, Fielder-Civil received his sentence: 27 months in jail.

In a continued downhill spiral, Winehouse was accused in September of hitting a female fan who had asked her to pose for a photograph in London. Winehouse was later acquitted of the charge.

BREAKING UP WITH BLAKE

Fielder-Civil had received a 27-month sentence, but prisoners often served only half their sentenced time. Because he had already served nine months awaiting sentencing, Fielder-Civil was released from prison in November 2008. He entered a required drug treatment program, but

▲ FIELDER-CIVIL IN NOVEMBER 2008, DURING THE BRIEF
TIME HE WAS OUT OF JAIL

he was sent back to jail just weeks later. He had
failed a drug test, violating the bail conditions
under which he had been let out. Winehouse
retreated for a vacation in the Caribbean's Saint
Lucia in January 2009 for a few months and was
reportedly looking better than she had in prior
months, but things were not on the upswing.

Around the time she left for vacation, the
imprisoned Fielder-Civil filed for divorce with

his lawyer, citing adultery on Winehouse's part. When Fielder-Civil first filed for the split, Winehouse announced she planned to contest the breakup. "Blake is the male version of me. We're perfect for each other," she said.[2] On a song called "Between the Cheats" recorded approximately a year before, Winehouse croons "I would die before I divorce ya."[3] The song appears on an album that was released after Winehouse's death. Fielder-Civil was released in February, and a British court granted the divorce six months later in July 2009. Winehouse admitted to the accused adultery in the divorce papers, but she was devastated by the breakup.

Quick Split

Neither Winehouse nor Fielder-Civil was present at the London High Court's Family Division when their divorce was declared official on July 16, 2009. Judge Michael Segal's proceedings lasted a matter of seconds, ending Winehouse and Fielder-Civil's tumultuous marriage that began in May 2007.

The couple's struggles with substance abuse, prison time, and infidelity were very public and had characterized Winehouse and Fielder-Civil's short, unstable marriage. But according to some friends, underlying love was beneath their tangle of problems. "I know they were really in love and they were soulmates," said Sarah Aspin, Fielder-Civil's romantic interest at the time of Winehouse's death. Although the love may have been there, the couple's problems proved insurmountable. "She always loved him and he always loved her—but it was just never going to work."[4]

While the legal process for the divorce was pending, Winehouse got into another situation requiring legal help. She returned to London in March 2009 and was promptly arrested by appointment for allegedly punching a fan at a Society Ball social event the past September. That arrest prevented Winehouse from leaving the United Kingdom for a planned performance at the Coachella Festival in Southern California. But she was cleared in time to return to the Caribbean and headline the Saint Lucia Jazz Festival that May.

Winehouse's performance in Saint Lucia was scheduled to take place days after she was hospitalized there for dehydration. But despite her hospitalizations and her track record, this time it was the weather, not Winehouse, that caused problems during her performances. The show was hindered by heavy rain and technical problems. The crowd booed when Winehouse walked off the stage six songs into the set. Though Winehouse looked disinterested during her abbreviated performance, her publicist said it was entirely because of weather that the show was cut short. "Amy would like to express her disappointment that weather forced the abandonment of her show," her spokesperson said the following day. "The set started well, but as the heavens opened, a number of technical difficulties occurred on stage."[5]

The Saint Lucia performance had been billed as Winehouse's big comeback, but it ended in frustration for both Winehouse and her fans. Then, Winehouse herself canceled a subsequent comeback show scheduled in London after again being hospitalized for dehydration.

That summer, her parents urged Winehouse publicly to seek help, claiming she had continued abusing alcohol even during her multiple stints in drug rehab. Even as she may have been gaining control of her drug use, Winehouse's continual alcohol abuse was becoming most concerning. "The need to rescue her is enormous," Janis told a British television station. "I just want her to be okay, and I would do whatever it took to make that right."[6]

Despite these struggles, Winehouse launched her own label, Lioness Records, in September 2009. The label

Drinking Danger

In a 2009 plea for their daughter to get help, Janis and Mitch commended Winehouse for making strides toward getting off drugs, but they pointed to alcohol as the greater danger at that stage. "For the last six months, there's been a remarkable recovery," Mitch said. "A gradual recovery, which is good. With slight backward steps [with alcohol]. . . . I need my daughter to be a whole person again."[7] Their concerned plea turned out to be a premonition of their daughter's death.

▲ WINEHOUSE RETURNING HOME FROM SAINT LUCIA IN 2009

was named after a necklace her grandmother Cynthia gave her. The label stayed close to home for its first release, *Introducing Dionne Bromfield*, which was the debut album from Winehouse's 13-year-old goddaughter. Mirroring her godmother, Bromfield's young voice showed great promise.

9

FINAL MONTHS

The 2009 holiday season was no time for celebration for the Winehouses. Mitch and Janis remained concerned about their daughter's erratic behavior and addictions, and Winehouse did nothing to alleviate their fears. On December 23, she was charged with assault and a public order offense—a crime that interferes with how society operates in public—for allegedly pulling a British theater manager's hair. The manager had tried to stop Winehouse from shouting profanities throughout a pantomime

▶ DESPITE HER FAMILY'S CONCERNS, WINEHOUSE CONTINUED LIVING A DESTRUCTIVE LIFESTYLE IN 2009.

of *Cinderella*. Pantomimes are fit-for-families theater performances based on nursery tales put on during the Christmas season, and Winehouse's outbursts were anything but kid friendly. In January 2010, Winehouse pleaded guilty to common assault and disorder for the incident. She had to pay a small fine and was given a two-year conditional discharge, which required her to stay out of trouble.

Many speculated that, given Winehouse's history, staying out of trouble for two years would be an impossible task. When it came to major brushes with the law, however, Winehouse was reasonably well behaved following the incident. What she could not escape were her ongoing substance-abuse problems.

A Clothing Line and Rehab

In early June 2010, a relatively healthy-looking Winehouse was spotted acting affectionately toward British film director Reg Traviss. Just a week later, London newspaper the *Sun* reported she was back in rehab after a bout of hard drinking. Around that same time, word got out that Winehouse had been working with British sportswear designer Fred Perry on a clothing line for 2010.

The Winehouse-Perry clothing line collaboration was formally announced in the October 14, 2010, issue of *Harper's Bazaar* magazine, which included an interview with Winehouse. In the interview, Winehouse indicated she was in a good place in her life. "If I died tomorrow, I would be a happy girl," she said, adding that she was dating a "nice boyfriend" who treated her well, referring to Traviss.[1] As for the clothing line, Winehouse said the invitation came as a terrific surprise. "I knew *exactly* what

Amy Winehouse for Fred Perry Collection

After releasing their collaborated collection in 2010, Winehouse and Perry began work to continue the line with a 2011 collection. The collection was still in the works when Winehouse died. The AW11 Amy Winehouse for Fred Perry Collection was released posthumously on August 8, 2011.

"Amy was passionate and dedicated to the collection," Perry said, "and her signature style is clearly stamped across each piece."[2] Winehouse embodied a 1950s look with her tall hairstyle, catlike eyeliner, and vintage dresses. The line's details bring Winehouse's style to life. According to the collection's official Web site,

Referencing Amy's love of 50s Americana and art deco Miami, the collection features an exclusive print scattered with Cadillacs, juke boxes and cats-eye sunglasses in a palette of pink mist, pale blue, and black.[3]

Perry noted that the royalties and fees from the 2011 collection would be donated to the Amy Winehouse Foundation, the charity set up by her family after she died.

I wanted," she said. "And I love Fred Perry *so much*. I was honored."[4]

FINAL SUCCESSES—AND FAILURES

While she was still trying to kick her addictions, Winehouse found mixed success onstage and in the studio. She contributed a well-reviewed cover of Lesley Gore's "It's My Party" to the November 2010 Quincy Jones tribute album, *Q: Soul Bossa Nostra*. Raved Jones, "Amy's talents are undisputable, and I am astounded not only by her voice but by her tremendous knowledge of and respect for music and its history."[5]

At Brazil's Summer Soul Festival in January 2011, Winehouse gave her first major performance since 2008. According to *Rolling Stone*, she was "in good form" as she sang her old material and new covers.[6] As she lounged in the sun between shows, Winehouse looked skinny but otherwise healthy. By performing in faraway locales—Brazil, Dubai, and the United Arab Emirates—Winehouse worked to regain her confidence while avoiding critical British fans and ferocious London tabloids.

Back in England on March 23, Winehouse made what would be her last trip to the studio. An energized recording session took place at the famous Abbey Road Studios that day with

▲ TONY BENNETT AND WINEHOUSE AT ABBEY ROAD
STUDIOS ON MARCH 23, 2011

85-year-old crooner Tony Bennett. Winehouse
and Bennett recorded "Body and Soul" for
Bennett's September 2011 album, *Duets II*.

"Body and Soul"

Singer Bennett, who sang with Winehouse at her last recording session, participated in a tribute to the late singer at the 2011 MTV Video Music Awards. He showed a video clip of the session when the two sang "Body and Soul" for his *Duets II* album. Bennett praised Winehouse for her talent, comparing her to jazz artists Ella Fitzgerald and Billie Holiday.

"Body and Soul," Winehouse's final recording, won the Grammy Award for Best Pop Duo/Group Performance of 2011. The album, *Duets II*, was also nominated and won for Best Traditional Pop Vocal Album.

"We had a beautiful time in the studio and I knew that Amy was happy with how she performed," Bennett said. "I thought she was brilliant."[7]

However, Bennett also told Reuters news agency afterward that during their recording session, Winehouse expressed serious concerns over her alcohol addiction and did not think she would live much longer. Bennett recalled,

She was in trouble at that time. What people didn't realize at that time, she really knew, and in fact I didn't really know it when we were making the record. . . . She knew she was in a lot of trouble, that she wasn't gonna live. And it wasn't drugs. It was alcohol.[8]

On May 25, Winehouse checked into the Priory Hospital North London for another try at controlling her substance abuse. She stayed in rehab only a week, but a representative said she had completed an assessment and was eager to begin her planned European tour. The tour was carefully managed by Winehouse's handlers, who informed the staff at each hotel to remove the minibar from her room.

But a disastrous opening show on June 18 in Serbia wound up being not only the first but also the last performance of the tour. Winehouse showed up more than an hour late, apparently drunk. She seemed to forget some lyrics, and she clutched her stomach and face before 20,000 fans, many of whom booed.

British journalist Chas Newkey-Burden described the scene in *Amy Winehouse: The Biography 1983–2011*:

> *She hugged herself and looked at turns confused, angry and sad. She made for a distressing sight. It was hard to believe that she had, in recent months, been doing so well. There was also an uncomfortable sense that we were seeing a reluctant*

Sad Performance in Serbia

Alternative singer Moby was slated to perform in Serbia along with Winehouse on June 18 and witnessed her troubled performance. Moby knew something was off as he arrived to perform. "The moment I got out of the car, I knew something was wrong," he told the *Hollywood Reporter*. "From backstage, I could hear the audience booing louder than the music."[9] Moby got sight of what was happening onstage and was shocked and saddened. "Amy was just standing there, swaying back and forth and mumbling occasionally," he said. "The band were playing quietly and looking uncomfortable and the audience was looking on in disbelief."[10]

star being forced to perform, perhaps thanks to the financial greed of others.[11]

The remainder of the tour was canceled. Winehouse would never again perform solo onstage.

———•◆•———

▲ WINEHOUSE IN BELGRADE, SERBIA, ON JUNE 18, 2011—
HER LAST TIME PERFORMING SOLO ONSTAGE

10

THE BATTLE ENDS

Clouds covered London on July 23, 2011. Many British music lovers were headed to Live Fest 2011, the city's largest indoor music festival. But the buzz around England would soon turn to a darker event—one that would sadden millions around the world. That afternoon, Winehouse was found dead in her London home at the age of 27.

Winehouse's live-in security guard told police he had checked on Winehouse twice on the morning of her death and found her sleeping. When he checked on her again at 3:00 p.m.,

▶ MITCH AND JANIS, GRIEVING THE LOSS OF THEIR DAUGHTER TWO DAYS AFTER HER DEATH

she was not breathing. Three empty vodka bottles were found in her room.

The day before she died, Winehouse had visited a doctor and had reportedly received a clean bill of health. Close friend and singer Kelly Osbourne said she had spoken with Winehouse the night before her body was found and did not sense any reason for alarm. "She seemed absolutely fine," Osbourne said. "I don't understand how this could have happened."[1] Janis saw Winehouse the day before she died and said she was concerned for her health, as she often was during the last several years of Winehouse's life. "She seemed a bit out of it," Janis said in the days following her

Friends, Family, and Fans Say Good-bye

Flowers, photos, letters, and signs began decorating Winehouse's Camden home in north London in the days following the singer's death. "We can't stop crying," said 15-year-old Rui Tsuzuki, who came from Japan with her mother, Mai, to pay homage to Winehouse. "We had to be here. We loved Amy so much."[2]

Close friends, family, and recording industry colleagues mourned Winehouse's death in a private London synagogue service on July 26, 2011. "Goodnight my angel," Mitch told mourners, to conclude what many described as a touching eulogy filled with humorous stories about his daughter. "Sleep tight. Mommy and Daddy love you ever so much."[3] Friend and singer Kelly Osbourne wore her hair in a beehive to the funeral in honor of Winehouse. The memorial service closed with the playing of Carole King's classic "So Far Away," and many sang along.

daughter's death. "But her passing so suddenly still hasn't hit me."[4]

THE WORLD MOURNS

As word of Winehouse's death began making the rounds on the Internet and television, sad statements started pouring in from all over the globe. In the hours following the tragedy, Winehouse's fans and peers spread the news of her death and posted tributes to her on social media sites Facebook and Twitter at breakneck speed. Most reactions were filled with sadness and grief. "My heart goes out to her family," Tweeted actress Demi Moore. "May her troubled soul find peace."[5] Singer Josh Groban tweeted, "Drugs took her gift, her soul, her light, long before they took her life. RIP Amy."[6]

The Recording Academy issued a statement praising Winehouse as one of the most talented musicians in the world. "Five-time Grammy winner Amy Winehouse was a dynamic performer and musician who seamlessly blended rock, jazz, pop, and soul and created a sound all her own," it noted. "She will forever be remembered for her immense talent, and her music will live on for generations to come."[7]

Singer Ronnie Spector, the former lead singer of the 1960s girl group the Ronettes, released a remake of "Rehab" in 2011 to benefit Daytop Village, a rehabilitation program. Spector said of Winehouse, "She had that freedom that we didn't have in the '60s—to write her own stuff and all that. She meant everything to me because she brought back the girl-group sound."[8]

Adele, one of the biggest forces in popular music at the time, pointed to Winehouse as a pioneer. "Amy paved the way for artists like me," Adele wrote on her blog, "and made people excited about British music again."[9]

In 2011, music superstar Lady Gaga expressed to *Rolling Stone* what Winehouse meant to her:

I'm a huge fan. She was my only hope when I was up and coming. Nobody knew who I was and I had no fans, no record label and everybody, when they met me, said I wasn't pretty enough or that my voice was too low or strange. They had nowhere to put me. And then I . . . remember thinking 'Well, they found somewhere to put Amy' . . . She just gave me a lot of hope.[10]

One Last Album

A new collection in her clothing line and her duet with Bennett were not Winehouse's only posthumous releases. Her own Lioness Records released a collection of unreleased songs Winehouse recorded over a nine-year period in December 2011. The album, *Lioness: Hidden Treasures* is technically Winehouse's third album.

▲ Fans flooded Winehouse's neighborhood, Camden Square, in the days following her death, leaving tributes near her home.

Alcohol Overdose

After months of speculation, an October coroner's report used a British legal term, misadventure, to indicate Winehouse had died of accidental causes. An alcohol binge was the culprit. It was determined that Winehouse, who stood only slightly taller than five feet (1.5 m), had more than five times the British legal driving limit of alcohol in her petite body at the time she died— the equivalent of 12 drinks. Many speculated that drugs played a role in Winehouse's death. According to the coroner's report, however, no illegal drugs were in her system at the time of her death. It was reported that the only drug in her system was a small trace of Librium—a legal drug used to treat alcohol withdrawal.

Not everyone reacted with shock to Winehouse's passing and how it happened. Some saw it as a predictable end for someone who refused to help herself despite numerous warning signs and close calls. Fashion consultant and television personality Tim Gunn said,

> *I have to say that as tragic as this is, you can't want someone to succeed unless that individual wants to, and she was on a downward spiral, and she resisted all help. . . . She's going to go down in history as [a] tragic icon.*[11]

However history treats the rise and fall of Winehouse in years and decades to come, hers will always be a tale of unique talent, personality, and a captivating but brief run of success. Winehouse's short life was a rollercoaster of lows

The Amy Winehouse Foundation

Winehouse's family created the Amy Winehouse Foundation to support vulnerable youth. It was launched on September 14, 2011—what would have been Winehouse's twenty-eighth birthday. Mitch said the foundation would try to help young people "who are in need by reason of ill health, disability, financial disadvantage, or addiction."[12]

▲ WINEHOUSE'S SHORT LIFE WAS FILLED WITH PASSION, TALENT, AND BITTER STRUGGLE, FOREVER PRESERVED IN THE MUSIC SHE LEFT BEHIND.

from drug and alcohol abuse and magnificent career highs. "When she wasn't drinking," her father said, "she was absolutely on top of the world."[13]

TIMELINE

1983

Amy Jade Winehouse is born on September 14 in London, England.

1992

Winehouse's parents, Mitch and Janis, separate due to Mitch having an ongoing affair.

1993

Winehouse enrolls in the Susi Earnshaw Theatre School in London but is either expelled or drops out within two years.

2003

Winehouse's debut album, *Frank*, is released in the United Kingdom on October 20.

2004

Winehouse begins drinking heavily, abusing drugs, and inflicting self-harm.

2006

Winehouse's single "Rehab" is released on October 23 and rises up the charts worldwide.

1996

Winehouse is accepted into the Sylvia Young Theatre School in London but drops out of school for good shortly after.

2002

Winehouse receives first a management contract, then a music publishing contract and a recording contract.

2003

Winehouse and Blake Fielder-Civil meet in a London bar and begin dating.

2006

Winehouse's second album, *Back to Black*, is released on October 27.

2007

Winehouse and Fielder-Civil marry in Miami, Florida, on May 18.

2007

Back to Black is the year's top-selling album in the UK with 1.85 million copies sold.

TIMELINE

2007

Winehouse reportedly checks in and out of rehab twice, leaving before she completes treatment.

2007

In November, Fielder-Civil is arrested to await trial on charges of alleged assault and bribery.

2008

On January 24, Winehouse checks into rehab.

2009

A London court grants Fielder-Civil and Winehouse a divorce on July 16.

2009

Winehouse launches her own label, Lioness Records, on September 21.

2011

Winehouse checks into the Priory Hospital North London on May 25 for alcohol rehab.

2008

Winehouse performs via satellite during the Grammy Awards on February 10.

2008

Winehouse wins five Grammys on February 10 for the album *Back to Black* and the single "Rehab."

2008

On July 21, Fielder-Civil is sentenced to 27 months in jail for the assault and attempted bribe of a British pub owner.

2011

On June 18, Winehouse's show in Serbia is canceled mid-performance. It is the last time Winehouse performs solo onstage.

2011

On July 23, 27-year-old Winehouse is found dead in her London home.

2011

Winehouse's family establishes the Amy Winehouse Foundation in September.

DATE OF BIRTH
September 14, 1983

PLACE OF BIRTH
London, England

DATE OF DEATH
July 23, 2011

PLACE OF DEATH
London, England

PARENTS
Mitch and Janis Winehouse

MARRIAGE
Blake Fielder-Civil (2007–2009)

CAREER HIGHLIGHTS

Albums
Frank (2003)
Back to Black (2006)
Lioness: Hidden Treasures (2011)

QUOTE

"I want people to hear my voice and just . . . forget their troubles for five minutes."—*Amy Winehouse*

GLOSSARY

acquitted
A complete discharge of an accusation in court.

cabaret
A nightclub or restaurant that provides entertainment while the audience eats or drinks.

chart
A weekly listing of the current best-selling records.

debut
A performer's first formal concert or recording.

demo
A collection of tracks that can be pitched to recording studios.

hip-hop
A style of popular music associated with US urban culture that features rap spoken against a background of electronic music or beats.

incoherent
Speaking in a way that is unclear and difficult for other people to understand.

jazz
An early-twentieth-century US music style developed from ragtime and blues that typically features improvisation.

posthumous
Something that happens or continues after a person dies.

producer
> Someone who oversees or provides money for a play, television show, movie, or album.

publicist
> A person who handles media relations or public relations for an artist.

record label
> A company that manages a band's music, particularly in regards to producing, manufacturing, distributing, and marketing albums.

rehab
> Short for rehabilitation; an effort to overcome an addiction to drugs or alcohol.

royalties
> Money given to an artist based on a percentage of sales.

track
> A portion of a recording that contains a single song or piece of music.

ADDITIONAL RESOURCES

SELECTED BIBLIOGRAPHY

Eliscu, Jenny. "The Diva and Her Demons: Rolling Stone's 2007 Amy Winehouse Cover Story." *Rolling Stone*. Rolling Stone, 23 July 2011. Web. 15 May 2012.

Newkey-Burden, Chas. *Amy Winehouse: The Biography*. London, UK: John Blake, 2008. Print.

Yaeger, Lynn. "Remembering Amy Winehouse." *Vogue*. Condé Nast, 25 July 2011. Web. 16 May 2012.

FURTHER READINGS

Morris, Andy, and Christina Westover. *Open Book: The Life and Death of Amy Winehouse*. Neptunes, 2011. Print.

O'Shea, Mick. *Amy Winehouse: A Losing Game*. London: Plexus, 2011. Print.

Winehouse, Mitch. *Amy, My Daughter*. New York: HarperCollins, 2012. Print.

WEB LINKS

To learn more about Amy Winehouse, visit ABDO Publishing Company online at **www.abdopublishing.com**. Web sites about Amy Winehouse are featured on our Book Links page. These links are routinely monitored and updated to provide the most current information available.

FOR MORE INFORMATION

For more information on this subject, contact or visit the following organizations.

Amy Winehouse Foundation
PO Box 66751, London, England, NW5 9FL
609-383-2323
www.amywinehousefoundation.org
The official Web site for the Amy Winehouse Foundation was started by Winehouse's family to connect with and help those in need who are suffering from addiction and mental health problems. Find information about Winehouse, upcoming events tied to the organization or her music, and contact information for several drug and alcohol addiction help groups. Donations can be made to the foundation online as well.

The Grammy Museum
800 W. Olympic Boulevard, Ste. A245, Los Angeles, CA 90015
213-765-6800
www.grammymuseum.org
The Grammy Museum features exhibits related to many genres of music. Visitors will find information on songs, albums, awards, and the lives of Winehouse and many other great singers. Special events and exhibits, an onsite store carrying memorabilia, and tours create a well-rounded experience for visitors.

Source Notes

Chapter 1. Live from London

1. Lynette Rice. "Amy Winehouse at 2008 Grammys: CBS Exec Reflects on a Moment to Remember." *EW.com*. Entertainment Weekly Inc., 23 July 2011. Web. 15 May 2012.

2. "Amy Winehouse to Perform via Satellite." *CNN Entertainment*. Cable News Network, 8 Feb. 2008. Web. 15 May 2012.

3. Associated Press. "Winehouse Dominates Grammys with 5 Wins." *Today Music*. MSNBC.com, 11 Feb. 2008. Web. 15 May 2012.

4. *Amy Winehouse, 1983–2011: A Tribute*. Commemorative Issue of *Time* Dec. 2011: 7. Print.

Chapter 2. Born into Music

1. Alun Palmer. "Amy Winehouse—a Talent Dogged by Self Destruction." *Mirror*. MGN Ltd, 25 July 2011. Web. 15 May 2012.

2. Ibid.

3. "Amy Winehouse's Tough Childhood." *Boston.com*. NY Times Co., 13 Mar. 2008. Web. 15 May 2012.

4. Ibid.

5. Jenny Eliscu. "The Diva and Her Demons: Rolling Stone's 2007 Amy Winehouse Cover Story." *Rolling Stone*. Rolling Stone, 23 July 2011. Web. 15 May 2012.

6. *Susi Earnshaw Theatre School*. Susi Earnshaw Theatre School, n.d. Web. 15 May 2012.

7. Ben Sisario. "Amy Winehouse, British Soul Singer With a Troubled Life, Dies at 27." *New York Times*. New York Times, 23 July. 2011. Web. 15 May 2012.

8. Mark Beech. "Amy Winehouse, Grammy-Winning Soul, Jazz Singer, Dies at 27." *Bloomberg*. Bloomberg L.P., 23 July 2011. Web. 15 May 2012.

Chapter 3. Songs Over School

1. "Amy Winehouse – Goals (video)." *Bio*. A&E Television Networks, n.d. Web. 15 May 2012.

2. Janet Mock and Julia Wang, eds. "Amy Winehouse." *People*. Time Inc., n.d. Web. 15 May 2012. 7 Dec. 2011.

3. Jenny Eliscu. "The Diva and Her Demons: Rolling Stone's 2007 Amy Winehouse Cover Story." *Rolling Stone*. Rolling Stone, 23 July 2011. Web. 15 May 2012.

4. Chas Newkey-Burden. *Amy Winehouse: The Biography*. London: John Blake, 2008. Print. 21–22.

5. Jenny Eliscu. "The Diva and Her Demons: Rolling Stone's 2007 Amy Winehouse Cover Story." *Rolling Stone*. Rolling Stone, 23 July 2011. Web. 15 May 2012.

6. Ibid.

7. Amanda Dobbins. "Read 17-Year-Old Amy Winehouse's Post-Fame To-Do List." *Vulture*. New York Media LLC, 28 Dec. 2010. Web. 15 May 2012.

8. Chas Newkey-Burden. *Amy Winehouse: The Biography*. London: John Blake, 2008. Print. 11.

9. Sheila Marikar. "Amy Winehouse: Five Facts You May Not Have Known." *ABC News*. ABC News, 27 July 2011. Web. 15 May 2012.

10. Jenny Eliscu. "The Diva and Her Demons: Rolling Stone's 2007 Amy Winehouse Cover Story." *Rolling Stone*. Rolling Stone, 23 July 2011. Web. 15 May 2012.

11. Ibid.

Chapter 4. Discovered

1. Jenny Eliscu. "The Diva and Her Demons: Rolling Stone's 2007 Amy Winehouse Cover Story." *Rolling Stone*. Rolling Stone, 23 July 2011. Web. 15 May 2012.

2. Steve Baltin. "Amy Winehouse Collaborator Talks Unreleased Songs, Demos." *Rolling Stone*. Rolling Stone, 2 Aug. 2011. Web. 16 May 2012.

3. Ibid.

4. Juliette Ashby. "About Juliette Ashby." *Juliette Ashby Official Website*. Juliette Ashby, n.d. Web. 16 May 2012.

5. Ibid.

Chapter 5. *Frank*

1. John Murphy. "Amy Winehouse—Frank (Island)." *MusicOMH*. OMH, 20 Oct. 2003. Web. 16 May 2012.

2. Matt Walton. "Amy Winehouse: Frank." *BBC Collective*. BBC, 17 Oct. 2003. Web. 16 May 2012.

3. Beccy Lindon. "Amy Winehouse, Frank." *The Guardian*. Guardian News and Media Limited, 16 Oct. 2003. Web. 16 May 2012.

4. "Amy Winehouse—Stronger Than Me." *YouTube*. YouTube, 23 Dec. 2009. Web. 16 May 2012.

5. Chas Newkey-Burden. *Amy Winehouse: The Biography*. London: John Blake, 2008. Print. 47.

6. Garry Mulholland. "Charmed and Dangerous." *The Guardian*. Guardian News and Media Limited, 31 Jan. 2004. Web. 16 May 2012.

7. Ibid.

8. Ibid.

9. Pete Lewis. "Amy Winehouse: Classic Interview (April 2004)." *Blues & Soul*. Blues & Soul Magazine. Apr. 2004. Web. 16 May 2012.

10. Garry Mulholland. "Charmed and Dangerous." *The Guardian*. Guardian News and Media Limited, 31 Jan. 2004. Web. 16 May 2012.

11. Ibid.

12. Pete Lewis. "Amy Winehouse: Classic Interview (April 2004)." *Blues & Soul*. Blues & Soul Magazine. Apr. 2004. Web. 16 May 2012.

Chapter 6. Love and Trouble

1. Chris Willman. "Voice of the Beehive." *EW.com*. Entertainment Weekly Inc., 18 May 2007. Web. 16 May 2012.

2. *Amy Winehouse, 1983–2011: A Tribute*. Commemorative Issue of *Time* Dec. 2011: 13. Print.

3. Ibid.

4. Anna Bahr. "Amy Winehouse Death: Blake Fielder Civil Singer Left Out Of Will." *The Huffington Post*. TheHuffingtonPost.com, Inc., 26 July 2011. Web. 16 May 2012.

5. Lynn Yaeger. "Remembering Amy Winehouse." *Vogue*. Condé Nast, 25 July 2011. Web. 16 May 2012.

6. Lara Salahi. "Amy Winehouse: Career Shadowed by Manic Depression." *ABC News*. ABC News Internet Ventures, 25 July 2011. Web. 16 May 2012.

7. Chris Lee. "Amy Winehouse's Dark Love Affair." *The Daily Beast*. The Newsweek/Daily Beast Company LLC, 24 July 2011. Web. 16 May 2012.

8. Liz Corcoran. "Parents Urge Amy Winehouse & Husband to Get Help." *People*. Time Inc., 28 Aug. 2007. Web. 16 May 2012.

SOURCE NOTES
CONTINUED

Chapter 7. Back to Black

1. J. Freedom du Lac. "That Winehouse Buzz? Believe It." *Washington Post*. Washington Post, 13 Mar. 2007. Web. 16 May 2012.

2. Ibid.

3. "Amy Winehouse—Rehab." *YouTube*. YouTube, 23 Dec. 2009. Web. 16 May 2012.

4. Kerri Mason. "Review: Amy Winehouse's Back to Black." *Billboard.com*. Rovi Corporation, 11 Mar. 2007. Web. 16 May 2012.

5. "Back to Black (Amy Winehouse): iTunes Review." *iTunes*. Apple Inc., n.d. Web. 16 May 2012.

6. "Amy Winehouse." *Saturday Night*. Saturday Night Magazine, n.d. Web. 16 May 2012.

7. Ibid.

8. Chas Newkey-Burden. *Amy Winehouse: The Biography*. London: John Blake, 2008. Print. 113.

9. Ibid. 114.

10. Alanah Eriksen. "'Amy and I Loved Each Other in an Unhealthy, Co-Dependent Way,' Says Winehouse's Ex-Husband Blake Fielder Civil." *Mail Online*. Associated Newspapers Ltd., 31 July 2011. Web. 16 May 2012.

11. Marisa Laudadio. "Amy Winehouse Treated For Exhaustion." *People*. Time Inc., 8 Aug. 2007. Web. 16 May 2012.

12. "Famously Exhausted Celebs." *Chicago Tribune*. Chicago Tribune, 16 Oct. 2010. Web. 16 May 2012.

13. "Stars' Extreme Body Battles." *The Sun*. News Group Newspapers Limited, n.d. Web. 16 May 2012.

14. Mike Collett-White. "Amy Winehouse Checks into Rehab Clinic." *Reuters*. Thomson Reuters, 24 Jan. 2008. Web. 16 May 2012.

15. Chas Newkey-Burden. *Amy Winehouse: The Biography*. London: John Blake, 2008. Print. 65–66.

Chapter 8. Fast Living

1. "Mama Winehouse: Amy 'On Road to Recovery.'" *E! Online*. E! Entertainment Television, LLC, 12 Feb. 2008. Web. 16 May 2012.

2. Simon Perry. "Amy Winehouse: 'I Won't Let Blake Divorce Me.'" *People*. Time Inc., 17 Jan. 2009. Web. 16 May 2012.

3. AFP. "Amy Winehouse: It's a Hard Knock Life." *The Express Tribune*. The Express Tribune News Network, 11 Dec. 2011. Web. 16 May 2012.

4. Adam Rathe. "Blake Fielder-Civil 'Devastated' over Ex-Wife Amy Winehouse's Death: 'I Can't Believe She's Dead.'" *New York Daily News*. NY Daily News.com, 25 July 2011. Web. 16 May 2012.

5. Daniel Kreps "Amy Winehouse's Comeback Gig Plagued By Problems." *Rolling Stone*. Rolling Stone, 11 May 2009. Web. 16 May 2012.

6. Breanne L. Heldman. "Amy Winehouse's Parents: She's Still Drinking, Needing Rescue." *E! Online*. E! Entertainment Television, LLC, 17 June 2009. Web. 16 May 2012.

7. Ibid.

Chapter 9. Final Months

1. Polly Vernon. "Amy Winehouse: Unplugged." *Harper's Bazaar*. Hearst Communications, 14 Oct. 2010. Web. 16 May 2012.

2. "Amy Winehouse Clothing Lines to be Released as Planned." *USA Today*. USA Today, 8 Aug. 2011. Web. 16 May 2012.

3. "Amy Winehouse." *Fredperry.com*. Fred Perry, n.d. Web. 16 May 2012.

4. Polly Vernon. "Amy Winehouse: Unplugged." *Harper's Bazaar*. Hearst Communications, 14 Oct. 2010. Web. 16 May 2012.

5. Daniel Kreps. "Amy Winehouse Records Quincy Jones Tribute." *Rolling Stone*. Rolling Stone, 9 Sep. 2010. Web. 16 May 2012.

6. Matthew Perpetua. "Video: Amy Winehouse Sings New Covers in Brazil." *Rolling Stone*. Rolling Stone, 10 Jan. 2011. Web. 16 May 2012.

7. Mark Beech. "Amy Winehouse, Tony Bennett Charity CD to Be Released Sept. 14." *Bloomberg*. Bloomberg L.P., 12 Sep. 2011. Web. 16 May 2012.

8. "Amy Winehouse Knew Alcohol Addiction Would Cause Her Death: Tony Bennett (Photos)." *International Business Times*. International Business Times, 30 Sep. 2011. Web. 16 May 2012.

9. Shirley Halperin. "Moby: 'I Was Horrified' at Winehouse's Final Show." *Today Music*. MSNBC.com, 25 July 2011. Web. 16 May 2012.

10. Ibid.

11. Chas Newkey-Burden. *Amy Winehouse: The Biography 1983–2011*. London: John Blake, 2011. Print. 219.

Chapter 10. The Battle Ends

1. "Amy Winehouse Dead for 'Several Hours' Before Paramedics Arrived: Had Seen a Doctor the Day Before." *International Business Times*. International Business Times, 25 July 2011. Web. 16 May 2012.

2. Amy Jones. "The Dark Side of the Amy Winehouse Vigil." *The Sun*. News Group Newspapers Limited, 1 Aug. 2011. Web. 16 May 2012.

3. Alison Schwartz and Monique Jessen. "Amy Winehouse Cremated After 'Moving Yet Humorous' Memorial Service." *People*. Time Inc., 26 July 2011. Web. 16 May 2012.

4. "Amy Winehouse Dead for 'Several Hours' Before Paramedics Arrived: Had Seen a Doctor the Day Before." *International Business Times*. International Business Times, 25 July 2011. Web. 16 May 2012.

5. The Associated Press. "Reaction to Death of Amy Winehouse." *Yahoo! News*. Yahoo, 23 July 2011. Web. 16 May 2012.

6. Ibid.

7. Ibid.

8. Mark C. Brown. "Ronnie Spector gives Amy Winehouse Her Due." *Reverb: the MSN Music Blog*. Microsoft, 29 July 2011. Web. 16 May 2012.

9. "Amy Flies in Paradise X." *Adele*. n.p. 25 July 2011. Web. 16 May 2012.

10. Patrick Doyle. "Exclusive: Lady Gaga Says 'Amy Deserved Better." *Rolling Stone*. Rolling Stone, 2 Aug. 2011. Web. 16 May 2012.

11. "The Associated Press. "Reaction to Death of Amy Winehouse." *Yahoo! News*. Yahoo, 23 July 2011. Web. 16 May 2012.

12. Mitch Winehouse. "Amy Winehouse Foundation." *Amy Winehouse Foundation*. n.p. n.d. Web. 16 May 2012.

13. Associated Press. "Amy Winehouse's Dad Says Seizure from Alcohol Detoxification Killed Daughter." *New York Daily News*. NY Daily News.com, 9 Sep. 2011. Web. 16 May 2012.

NDEX

ABOUT THE AUTHOR

David Aretha has authored more than 40 books for young readers, including *Eminem: Grammy-Winning Rapper*. He counts *The Beatles: Fifty Fabulous Years* among the dozens of books he has edited.

PHOTO CREDITS

Vince Bucci/Getty Images for MTV, cover, 3; Rex Features via AP Images, 7, 13, 17, 63, 67, 73, 87, 96 (top), 98 (top, bottom); Peter Macdiarmid/Getty Images for NARAS, 11; Rex USA, 15, 21, 23; Matt Dunham/AP Images, 28, 52, 69; Ian Dickson/Redferns/Getty Images, 31; nito/Shutterstock Images, 34; J. Quinton/FilmMagic/Getty Images, 37; David Butler/Rex USA/Everett Collection, 39; Mirrorpix/Everett Collection, 42; Adrian Seal/FilmMagic/Getty Images, 45; Dave Hogan/Getty Images, 47; Press Association/AP Images, 50; Matt Kent/WireImage/Getty Images, 54; John Shearer/WireImage/Getty Images, 57, 96 (bottom); Featureflash/Shutterstock Images, 61, 97; Wayne Starr/Express Newspapers/AP Images, 77; Sylvia Linares/FilmMagic/Getty Images, 79; Mark Allan/AP Images, 83; Sean Dempsey/PA/AP Images, 89; dutourdumonde/Shutterstock Images, 93, 99; Matt Cardy/Getty Images, 95